Table of Contents

Introduction

Congratulations on purchasing <u>Potty Training in A Weekend</u>: The Step-By-Step Guide to Potty Train Your Little Toddler in Less Than 3 Days. Perfect for Little Boys and Girls. Bonus Chapter with Tips for Careless Dads Included and thank you for doing so.

The following chapters will discuss the step-by-step instructions to potty train your child in just three days. Going beyond the bare minimum, this book covers not only just the physical steps that will need to be taken but also the mental preparation that will ensure that both you and your child are set up for success! This book will dispel the myths and misconceptions surrounding the potty training process and will outline how parents and caregivers can use psychology to make the potty training process more teamwork and less brute force. By following the system outlined here, potty training will be a shared goal that both parents and/or caregivers and their children will want to achieve together!

Not only will parents and caregivers benefit from learning how to create a spirit of teamwork during the process, but parents and caregivers will also learn how to handle the potty training outliers when potty training is not going as it should. Learning how to best support children in a variety of scenarios is an important part of potty training successfully and in a healthy manner.

To set the reader of this book up for success, it is important to begin with a strong knowledge base of the physiological and psychological processes behind potty training, or potty learning from the child's perspective. In other words, parents and caregivers need to know the physical and emotional processes at work during this period of time in order to best support their children through it. A brief note to the reader: Be prepared to hear some "potty talk" in this book! It is both necessary and healthy to be able to use accurate bathroom-related terminology during this process. Ultimately you will choose what terminology you use with your child, but for the purposes of this book it will be important to use bathroom-related language, so be prepared.

In addition to the real-life advice found throughout this book, there is also a bonus chapter that includes potty training tips and tricks from real-life dads fordads still in the trenches! All too often, books aimed at parents and caregivers forget that fathers are an Important part of this team, and the unique relationship they have with their children can be utilized in specific endeavors like this for ultimate success for everyone.

There are plenty of books on this subject on the market, thanks again for choosing this one! Every effort was made to ensure it is full of as much useful information as possible, please enjoy it!

Chapter 1: In the Beginning

As you prepare yourself to begin the process of potty training with your child, there are techniques that you can use to prepare both yourself and your child to set yourselves up for ultimate success during this process! A significant part of this preparation will be the mental preparation because the mindset that both you and your child enter into this endeavor with will largely determine how quickly you are successful. The process of preparing yourself and your child mentally for the new journey you are undertaking is called priming, and it is going to play a huge part in helping your potty training process run smoothly.

To begin, you must prime yourself to approach potty training in a healthy and practical manner. Sadly, according to the American Academy of Pediatrics, the premier children's health governing body in the United States of America, the developmental experience that has the most potential for abuse of children is potty training and it is easy to imagine why. Frustrations are understandable during potty training as pressure is high for everyone: parents, caregivers, and trainees! It will be important that parents and caregivers understand how to best manage their expectations and any frustrations that may come up during the process.

Parents and caregivers are understandably anxious during the potty training process as there is truly only so much that a parent or caregiver can do. It is always ultimately up to the child if they are ready to ditch their diapers or not, and this is not likely an intentional choice on the part of the child as much as it is just the result of their developmental reality at that moment.

In addition to this, parents and caregivers are also under the additional burden of the actual work involved in potty training. While most parents and caregivers are more than ready to shuck the diapers to the curb for the additional ease and freedom of having a toilet-trained child, the reality is that there will be much more work coming down the pike before the child is fully potty trained. Before the child is fully potty trained, there will be plenty of accidents and additional laundry, as well as the extra mental and physical work of setting timers and organizing and developing a game plan that involves potty schedules and schematics for rewards and reinforcement!

Children feed off of this anxiety and pressure as they

often recognize the importance of this monumental task being placed in front of them. This has the potential to create power struggles around toilet use, and nobody wants that! It is understandable that children will act out and push back against this pressure and anxiety, and this is what can lead to unacceptable and even dangerous uses of force from parents and caregivers as unnecessary and unproductive punishments intended to manipulate their children's behavior.

Careful examination of the expectations that parents and caregivers hold over their children's capabilities as well as a solid game plan to complete the potty training process will help to set the parent and/or caregiver up for success with their children.

Some of the expectations that parents and caregivers hold around the potty training process are a result of myths and misconceptions around the practice that have been around for many, many years that we will cover now.

Myth #1

There is a magic potty training age that if a parent and/or caregiver begins, the child will be more successful in the potty training process.

Fact

Every child develops according to their own schedule! Potty training is not an exact science because every child will have their own distinctly unique timetable as to when their mind and body is ready will be ready to begin the process. There is no need to put extra pressure on the process by ignoring the signs and signals your child is showing you as to whether or not they are ready to begin potty training just because the calendar says so! Most children potty train sometime between the ages of two and four, with outliers that begin younger than two and those that are still training beyond the age of four.

Myth #2

Potty training is something parents do to and for their children, not with their children.

Fact

This is as wrong as wrong can be! Potty training is not something that a parent and/or caregiver can do for their child, it is an interactive process that requires cooperation and teamwork from both parent and/or caregiver and child. You want your child to be your partner in this venture!

Myth #3

Your child is being willfully disobedient if they won't potty train according to your schedule and expectations.

Fact

While it could be true that your child is willfully pushing potty training away, this does not necessarily mean that your child is being disobedient. As was discussed in the introduction, there are many reasons why you cannot force a child to potty train before they are ready. There are physical and mental processes that must be developed before a child can fully learn the skill of proper toilet use.

Myth #4

If you've already potty trained an older sibling using a specific method, then the younger siblings should also be able to train using that method.

Fact

Each child is their own unique and individualistic person with their own personal needs and capabilities. Each child develops in their own time and what may have worked for their older sibling (or their cousin, or neighbor, or playmate) may not necessarily work for them.

Myth #5

Once my child potty trains, there is no looking back!

Fact

This is a very common myth. It is not accurate, however. Most children do go on to have accidents for some time after potty training. The window for becoming a potty pro is quite wide for small children, with some children having accidents up to a few years after they officially "potty train" and ditch their diapers. This is very normal. There is much to distract small children and it can be very easy to forget all about their bodily functions when they are learning so much every day about this dazzling new world all around them!

Myth #6

If we potty train our child to use the toilet during the day, we should potty train our child to stay dry throughout the night, too.

Fact

There are schools of thought regarding potty training that believe that potty training should be an "all or nothing" sort of experience, and this includes getting rid of any sort of diaper or pull-up type of training pants at nighttime. However, potty training at night is actually a completely different process than the process for potty training during the day because a child's ability to stay dry throughout the night has less to do with learning proper toileting habits and bodily signals and more to do with night time hormones related to urine production and the degree to how heavily your child sleeps. Most doctors and urologists agree that nighttime bladder control is not an issue until the child is around seven years old.

As you can see, there are many myths and misconceptions surrounding the potty training experience that can set a parent and/or caregiver up for expectations that can't be met. Sometimes this is a result of failing to recognize what potty learning truly is for the child.

For a child that has been diapered since birth, learning how to ditch their diapers requires a whole world of complexity that parents and caregivers often do not take the time to consider. For their tiny little bodies and minds, they have never had to pay much attention to their elimination habits. They've always just had their waste products exit their bodies when it needed to, without any real consideration or effort on their parts. To begin the potty training process, parents and caregivers must realize that they are essentially starting from scratch!

The child must first learn to be aware of her body and its functions. This requires an awareness that what is consumed will need to then exit the body as a waste product eventually. For some children, this is a surprise! Taking the time to help teach them this connection is an important building block in the potty training process. They need to understand that the juice box they just drank will be ready to come out within the next hour or so, and this will be an important part of the methodology in Chapter 2 when you are introduced to the steps of the three-day potty training method.

In addition to being aware that what comes in must go out, children must then learn to be aware of what it feels like *before* they need the toilet. Again, they have never needed to be aware of the sensation of a full bladder in need of emptying in their life, their bodies have just released whenever they needed to without any help or awareness on the part of the child. This process of paying attention to the body and learning to associate the sensations of their body with the need to sit on the potty chair is often one of the most aggravating aspects of potty training for both the child and their parents and/or caregivers.

One way to facilitate your child's learning about their bodily functions and the awareness of when they need to visit the restroom is to model this for them with your actions. This would include announcing to your child when you need to use the restroom and using descriptive language that they will understand. You will know your child best, but this could sound something like, "Oh, I think that glass of water I just drank is ready to come out! My bladder feels full, I need to pee/urinate/whatever terminology you choose," and you would say this while perhaps poking one finger into your lower abdomen over your bladder. Or perhaps you might say, "Oh, my stomach hurts a little bit down here,

I need to poop/defecate/whatever terminology you choose," and you would also say this while motioning to your lower abdomen. The point here is to help your child learn where these parts of their body are so they can begin to associate these areas with making a trip to the potty. You are also teaching them the language they will need during their potty training experience.

The other crucial element here is in modeling the actual process for our children. Children are visual creatures, and they love to do what they see others doing! For most children, their primary caregivers and/or parents are their primary models of behavior and being allowed to see a parent and/or caregiver sit on the toilet and go through the process themselves can give them a clear example of how they're supposed to do it. It is also important here to narrate the process for your little one, like this: "Okay, I have to pee now so I'm going to the potty. I'm going to pull my shorts down and sit here on the potty. Okay…. Now I just need to let my pee out! There it is, can you hear it? That's my pee going into the toilet! Alright, now I can grab a little bit of toilet paper, just like this, and wipe myself clean. Now I just need to toss it in the potty, pull my shorts back up, and flush! Ready to hear the toilet flush? Here it goes and WOO! Alright, now I get to wash my hands! I like this soap, it's blue. Pretty cool, right?"

Notice in the narrative above that the parent and/or caregiver is not only narrating each part of the experience, but they are also making the entire experience sound like fun! Children will want to also be able to mimic this experience, especially aspects like flushing the toilet. The entire experience needs to be described like it is something that is a great part of growing up. This is a part of priming the experience for your child. If the experience is primed as something fun and attractive, your child will join you in this quest rather than resist you.

In addition to this physical learning about the parts of your child's body and their awareness of them and what they do, there is a cognitive aspect that is required in potty training. Children must be able to not only feel the sensation of a full bladder or a bowel movement, but they must also be able to reason and rationalize with themselves to a certain extent. Young children often struggle with this part of the potty training process because it can be difficult for them to understand and engage in delayed gratification or time awareness. If a child is playing with their favorite toy in the living room, it won't matter too much if they feel the pressure of a full bladder and understand what that means if they don't have the cognitive skills yet to understand that they can set the toy down to go to the restroom and then come back for the toy again. For young children, they live in the moment, every moment. This cognitive awareness is one of the most crucial aspects of potty training and one of the reasons why so many of the "potty training tips and tricks" geared towards young toddlers do not work. A very young toddler simply will not have this cognitive awareness down enough to be able to make this choice, and this can lead to serious bladder and bodily issues when they are trained to hold their waste anyway.

This is why pediatrician and urologist groups caution against enforcing any potty training protocol before a child is displaying at least the following signs of readiness: able to communicate their need to use the toilet either verbally or nonverbally, can physically get themselves to the restroom safely and efficiently by either walking or crawling, can dress and undress themselves to use the toilet, and can sit safely on a toilet seat unassisted. Enforcing a potty training program before a child is ready can result in urinary tract infections, kidney damage, constipation, and a lifetime of poor toileting habits.

Parents and caregivers can assess if their child is cognitively prepared to begin the potty training process by gauging how much interest and self-awareness the child has around all things potty related. Ask yourself the following questions to see if your little one is cognitively prepared for potty training!

- Does your child express interest in the toilet by following family members into the restroom or commenting on "going potty" when it is mentioned?

- Does your child express interest in "being a big kid" and want to do what older siblings and older children do?

- Does your child express when their diaper is soiled by pulling on the wet/dirty diaper, trying to remove it or even removing it themselves, and/or announcing that they need a diaper change?

If you answered yes to all three of these questions, then

it is very likely that your child is cognitively prepared to begin the potty training process! Ask yourself the following questions to see if your little one is physically prepared for potty training!

- Is your child able to verbally and nonverbally express their physical needs, such as by asking for something to drink when thirsty or by stating they are cold and need a sweater?

- Is your child able to physically get themselves, without assistance, to the toilet and back by crawling or walking?

- Is your child able to dress and undress themselves efficiently enough to do so in the restroom largely unassisted?

- Is your child able to safely sit unassisted on a toilet or potty chair?

If you answered yes to all of these questions, then it is very likely that your child is physically prepared to begin the potty training process!

Once your child is demonstrating the cognitive and physical signs of readiness for potty training, then you can safely move on to the three-day potty training system! But first, a few words on the mental preparation moving forward.

You and your child will need to be a team in this endeavor. Not only is this necessary because one person cannot force another person to use a toilet (not safely and respectfully, anyway!) but it is also a matter of simple psychology.

Toddlers want to please their parents and caregivers-although it may not always seem like it! This perception happens because, for so much of those early childhood years, children have little to no bodily autonomy or control over where they go or what they do. This leaves them very few opportunities to assert their independence and capabilities in a healthy and constructive manner. This often translates then to what adults often view as being "petty" demands and tantrums, such as may occur over what color cup the child wants to drink out of or whether the child wants to put on their shoes or not.

Step back a moment and try to look at it from this tiny person's perspective for a moment: If you had no control over what time you woke up in the morning, what you had available to eat, no capabilities to perform the majority of the tasks being performed around you (cooking, driving, talking on the phone, etc) and little to no choice over how you spend your days, wouldn't you also on occasion feel the need to make a choice of your own, on your own terms, no matter how trivial it may seem to others? This is the perspective of the small child, and the more that parents and caregivers can explore and understand this, the better they will be able to work with their child's psychology so that everyone can experience a win.

This is where the psychology behind team building comes in. Parents and caregivers don't need the potty training process to be any more difficult than what it already will be and should take all the help they can get! This includes the help of their small child, and it begins with how the child is approached with the process of potty training.

The child should never be made to feel as if potty training is an event that is coming up that they will be forced to be a part of, but rather should feel as if they are making the decision to begin potty training. This is easy enough to do for most children between the ages of two and four because this age range is typically in the "I want to do it all by myself" mentality as they are looking to develop more of the autonomy and independence, they see being exercised by older people around them.

A note to parents and caregivers on how they speak to one another about the potty training process: Watch how you are wording your conversations within earshot of your small child. Keep in mind that children are almost always listening, even when they appear busy at play.

Comments that may not seem like much of a big deal can play into negative perspectives about the potty training process when heard by young ears that don't entirely understand what it all means. An example of this might sound something like, "We plan on <voice dropping conspiratorially> *potty training* this weekend," or "I just hope it's nothing like <insert name of child's playmate here> because their mom told me it was absolutely miserable! They spent months fighting it." This is even more of an issue for those comments that are made between parents and caregivers where there is visible negative body language such as head shaking, eye-rolling, or whispering behind hands.

Children are more aware of these social cues than parents and caregivers often assume, and this is not a good way to prime the potty training experience for your child!

In the interest of setting up the experience of potty training as a shared goal and shared effort, look around for examples of meaningful models that your child may use for potty training. Is there an older sibling that they look up to? Is there maybe an older neighbor that is close to the family? Or perhaps a favorite cartoon character?

Remember, you want your child to *want* to potty train, otherwise, it will be you trying to *force* your child to complete this developmental process, and this rarely works. Think about other developmental leaps that children take such as crawling, walking, and even talking. Has any parent and/or caregiver ever succeeded in forcing a baby to crawl? Is there any physical way to force a baby to walk when they simply don't have the leg and core strength and coordination between their body parts? How about forcing a baby to walk that simply doesn't have any interest in it yet because they still prefer to crawl? No, of course not.

Just as we encourage our children to learn to talk by modeling it for them and engaging with them verbally in a fun way, we can do the same with the developmental process of potty training.

Keeping this in mind, enlist the help of the meaningful models that you know your child will look up to and want to emulate. If it is an older sibling, ask the older sibling to join in on the modeling of bathroom behavior by both physically modeling the process and narrating in a fun and upbeat way. The older sibling can even say things like, "someday you will be able to do the potty just like me! Isn't that cool?"

If your child's meaningful model is a neighbor, you can ask the neighbor to announce before they have to run to the restroom, saying in an excited voice, "I have to go to the potty now, I'll be right back to keep playing with you in just a moment!" This would model both the process of making the decision to go to the toilet and also the idea that you can take a quick break from playing to go to the restroom and come right back to it.

If your child's meaningful model is a beloved cartoon character, then use that! There are a variety of ways that you can make this happen. There are many cartoon character toys that demonstrate the potty process and even sing cute little songs about going to the restroom, and they are available from major retailers; a quick google search will reveal what is available in that department.

There are also several cartoon episodes dedicated to teaching children how to go to the potty, and these are available in many different streaming services such as Netflix, Hulu, Amazon Prime, and PBS Kids, to name a few. They are also largely available via a quick google search, so do take advantage of that!

One children's show that is renowned for its successful induction of children into the potty training experience is PBS Kids' Daniel Tiger's Neighborhood and their episode, "Daniel Goes to the Potty." This episode features the beloved main character, Daniel Tiger, learning to go sit on the potty. The song that Daniel sings every time he feels the urge to go to the potty is incredibly catchy and memorable and has been used successfully by many a parent and caregiver to remind a child that they need to go sit on the potty!

If you are a screen-free family and have no interest in using media to help during the potty training process, then feel free to be creative and make up your own potty training song for your little one to sing! The catchier, the better. Make it something fun and upbeat that your child and you enjoy singing every time they need to go sit on the potty. This is a part of keeping the experience fun and upbeat. It's amazing what our children will do in pursuit of light-hearted fun with their parents and caregivers!

To further prime the potty training experience for your child, you can determine how to best set up your restroom for your child. Many parents and caregivers choose to use an independent potty chair, which is the small, child-size potty that can be purchased at any major retailer/big box store or online. An advantage of this is the safety feature of it being their perfect size and situated firmly on the ground. There is also a feeling of pride in ownership that many children feel when they have their very own little potty, just for them to use. Some parents even take their children with them to the store to pick out their very own potty chair or give them stickers to decorate the potty chair and make it their own.

Another option is to purchase one of the seat modifiers

that are also available through any major retailer and big box store or online that either attaches to the regular toilet seat or can be easily placed on top that makes the toilet seat a more child-friendly size. There are a few advantages to this, such as if bathroom space is limited and there is simply no room for another potty chair in the same room. Some children even prefer this option over the standalone child-size potty chair because they feel like more of a "big kid" with this option, and this seems to be the case more often when there is an older sibling as the child's meaningful model.

Another option that is similar to the seat modifier is to simply add a safety stool for the child so they can more easily get up on the regular toilet themselves. Often times this option can even be found with a hand-rail so they have something to keep their balance while climbing on and off. An advantage of this particular option is that it fulfills the same desire of the child to feel like a "big kid" in using the regular potty, and it also teaches them the necessary skills to navigate the regular-sized toilets they will find outside of the home. This can be very helpful for some children that may be uneasy about moving from the child-size options at home to the regular size toilets that they will find while using the restroom outside of the home.

Whatever potty option you choose, be sure to tailor it to your child and their needs. If you know that doing it "just like the big kids do" is going to be a big motivator, then perhaps it might be best to go with the options that modify the standard size toilet. If you know that your child doesn't like sitting on full-size chairs as well as smaller child-size chairs, then perhaps the child-size potty chair is best. If you know your child is always excited to sit in regular-sized chairs to be "like a big kid" then using the regular toilet with a safety addition might be the right incentive for them.

Your shopping trip also needs to include some favorite beverage options for your child. This is important because you will need to have your child drinking plenty of fluids during the three-day potty training weekend. This is to ensure that your child is experiencing a full bladder and the sensations that come along with it as you teach your child to associate that sensation with the need to go sit on the toilet. Parents often opt for both regular favorites and "special" beverages that the child rarely gets so there will be no question as to if the child will be interested in drinking them. You know your child best, but fruit juices, lemonades, or any sort of sweet beverage is usually always a hit with any small child!

The next thing to gather in preparation for your three-day potty training process is the underwear that your child will be replacing their diapers with! Many children really get a kick out of picking out their "big kid" underwear, so take them shopping with you. This also plays into the pride of ownership psychology, in which you want your child to feel like they have some control here, too. Really have fun with this, talk it up at the store and make it exciting and fun to get to pick out underwear with their favorite characters, colors, and patterns on them. Remember, this is all a part of priming the experience for your child!

Pro tip from a parent that has been there, done that: However, many pairs you think you need to start off with, double it. At the very least, double it! It is very likely that you will need them- and then some- during your potty training weekend extravaganza, so prep yourself well here!

Another important shopping trip that must take place

before the three-day potty training process is the trip in which you procure the treats and rewards that you will use to keep your child associating potty use with celebration and reward. Parents and caregivers will know their children best, but whatever you do, diversify your treat and reward supplies!

Some common ideas for treats and rewards that are often used during the potty training process are small candies such as skittles, smarties, or M&Ms that allow for sweet, exciting treats to be doled out just a couple at a time. Stickers with favorite cartoon and storybook characters on them and little puzzle and workbook-style books that your child can interact with are always a big hit! Some parents and caregivers like to create a treasure box of sorts for the potty training experience that the child gets to pick out after they've had a successful trip to the potty, and this is often filled with a variety of sweet treats and small prize style toys. Dollar stores often provide a great value for this avenue, as you can buy many little exciting "treasures" for the child that won't break the bank! Anything that is new and different is typically enough to incentivize a child to want to participate in the potty training process so they can earn their rewards!

Some parents and caregivers choose to share the treasure box with the child the day before the potty training process kicks off by letting the child take a peek and know that tomorrow, they will get a chance to check it out and pick items out for themselves when they use the big-kid potty. This gives them an element of excitement to associate with the big day!

Before the child heads off to bed the night before the potty training weekend, you can let them know that tomorrow you will be throwing away the diaper they are wearing and they will get to wear their big kid underwear and try the big kid potty! Let them know they will get to pick prizes out of the treasure box every time they pee or poop on their potty and that you will be right there with them to celebrate with them. Make sure they hear that you are excited for the next day and you are confident that you guys will have a great day. Let your child drift off to sleep imagining the exciting things awaiting them the next day!

In order to successfully utilize the Potty Training in A Weekend methodology, it is important to have a three-day long weekend devoted exclusively to the potty training process. This means that there need to be three days dedicated to the potty training process. No trips to the park, no running to the grocery store, no guests in the house to distract the parent and/or caregiver, and if you can swing it, siblings either 100% on board with helping be a part of this process or spending the long weekend out at a friend's house. The only thing you and your child should be doing over the course of this three-day weekend will be sharing this potty training experience!

Parents and caregivers that have been there and done that during this process recommend ensuring that you have the laundry and other household chores caught up, including meal planning and prepping so that your mind can remain exclusively focused on the task at hand. There will be accidents- make sure you're not the cause of them because you were distracted taking care of some household chore!

The Potty Training in A Weekend method has gained steadily in popularity over the course of the last decade, particularly in Western countries, with varying degrees of difference in each guide. The guide provided in this book is set up in such a way that you can learn about the many variances to this methodology and choose to adopt what you believe will work best for you and your little one. Just as every child is uniquely individual, so too is the home setup and the pattern of each individual household. View the guide here as a buffet of sorts: choose what you like and leave the rest.

Your results will vary because every child is an individual, but Potty Training in A Weekend method, when approached in a focused and mindful manner on the part of the parent and/or caregiver, is guaranteed to provide a bedrock foundation for your child's potty training prowess. Your goal should not be a 100% accident-free, potty using a child at the end of this weekend, but rather a child who is well on their way to becoming one.

Now that you have done the setup work to prime both yourself and your child to have the best mindset going into this process, you are ready to begin to delve into the step by step guide of potty training in a weekend.

Chapter 2: Potty Training in A Weekend

Day 1: Welcome to the Big Day!

Wake up and get yourself set up immediately with timer reminders before you even wake your child up for the day. Most people choose to use their smartphone for this, but if you do not have a smartphone, then any clock, watch or another electronic device that has a timer and alarm capability will do! It is best if it is a timer that is portable and you can move around with you as you move around your home, but if you are using a stationary alarm such as a microwave or stovetop, then just be aware of keeping the volume down on other electronics and outside noise throughout the day so you can hear the alarm.

The alarm will cue you to each and every time that you will need to take your child to sit on the potty. This should be approached as an exciting, fun thing for the first day. Every time the alarm sounds, react as if you are thrilled to be hearing it. Your child will catch on to this and be happy to hear it, too.

Your first alarm needs to be set for exactly 15 minutes after your child gets set up for the day, so set that up as you go in to get your child out of bed. Building on what you began the day before, get your child out of bed in a fun and playful manner, reminding them of the exciting day you two have planned!

Keep your language here simple and direct so as not to confuse your child too much on what the day will contain. A sample script might sound something like this: "Today you get to start using the big kid potty just like <insert meaningful model here>! You get to wear big kid underwear and when you go big kid potty today, you'll get to pick a prize out of the treasure box! Let's take off this soggy diaper and pick out some big kid underwear!"

A lot of parents make a big production out of tossing this "last wet diaper" into the trash with their child and some even have the child toss it out and say something along the lines of "bye-bye diapers! I'm a big kid now!"

Let your child pick out their own underwear to wear and be sure that you comment on how fun it is to have underwear with their favorite character, pattern, or print on it. You can comment on the softness of the material or the colors found on it. At some point during putting the underwear on, remind your child that underwear is not a diaper and that it is not meant to be peed or pooped in. Be sure to include something along the lines of, "do you feel like such a big kid with your big kid underwear on?"

Regarding the type of clothing your child should wear during this intensive potty training weekend, the only real requirement is that it needs to be something that your child can easily remove to sit on the potty. Many parents choose to just use an underwear and t-shirt combo, but anything that slides down and then back up easily will work. You don't want anything complicated that requires buttoning, zipping, or even Velcro because you don't want there to be any additional steps that your child will need to take to sit on the potty. You want to encourage as much independent movement as you can for your child around the potty. You want to help foster any associations between feeling capable and in control and use of the potty that you can.

Once you have gotten your child into their big kid underwear, it is time to begin the potty training process in earnest! Going into breakfast mode, allow your child to help you pick out what they would like for breakfast and announce to them they get to have a special drink since it is the morning, they begin their potty training process. Give them one of their favorite beverages that you have picked out from the store and encourage them to drink up. Let them know that they are going to fill their belly up with their special drink and then be able to go sit on the big-kid potty. Once your child begins to drink, set the alarm for 15 minutes. This will be the first time you put your child on the potty, and hopefully, the sugary drink will have done the trick. Let your child know that when the alarm goes off, they will be able to go in and sit on the big kid potty!

Once the first fifteen-minute alarm sounds, this will be your time to really play up the event. React to the alarm as if it is the most exciting thing you have ever heard. Lead your child into the restroom (or depending on their excitement level, they can lead you!) and narrate the process as you go. "Alright! Here we go, off to your big kid potty. I'm so excited for you! This is great. Here we are, to the bathroom. Okay, can you pull your big kid underwear down, *all by yourself*? Awesome! Okay, now you can climb up to sit on your potty. Okay! Now let's check-in, see if there's any pee-pee in there that you can put in the potty! <Show your child how to gently poke and put pressure on their lower abdomen, above their bladder> Do you feel some pee-pee in there? Let's see if you can put it in the potty!!!"

The cycle of drinking a beverage and then heading to the restroom will be repeated throughout this first day, but one of the most important aspects of this ritual will be in the narrative that you provide during this process. You want to continue to provide the child with the physical cues of where they will be feeling the pressure of their bladder, so they will make the association between the sensations of a full bladder and going to sit on the toilet.

For this first day, you will react with a celebration during every single visit to the potty. You want your child to experience a positive reinforcement of the association that going to the potty equals fun and happiness. It is not necessary that your child actually uses the potty chair, today you are celebrating just making the trip! You will celebrate each and every time they sit.

Allow your child two to three minutes to sit each time. During this time, stay with them. You can read a book about using the potty, listen to or sing a song about using the potty, or watch one of the episodes about potty training available on various forms of media. Again, you are working to train your child to associate the sensations of a full bladder and pressure in their abdomen with the experience of sitting on the potty. Remember that you are building these connections from the ground up because they have never had to build them before! They have to move from mindless and passive elimination to conscious and mindful recognition and decision-making.

Again, this first day your child will get to pick a new treat from the treasure box each and every time they sit on the potty, regardless of if they go to the bathroom in the toilet or not. This first day is only for creating positive associations and teaching both toileting habits and how to be aware of their bodily sensations.

An Important Note About Accidents

Accidents will happen over the course of this weekend, especially on the first day. Do not be discouraged! Treat each accident as a neutral incident and keep your emotions level. Do not react as if it is a disappointment or a failure of any kind. A sample script for this scenario might be, "Ooops, it looks like you didn't make it to the big kid potty. Let's go take this wet/dirty underwear over here and get all cleaned up. Next time, we will try to make it to the potty in time!"

Keep your narrative around potty accidents neutral and matter of fact. This is going to be a normal and natural part of the process and your child will be learning that when they go to the bathroom in their big kid underwear, it is a different sensation than when they went to the bathroom in their absorbent diaper.

Your child is making lots of new connections this weekend, one connection that they do NOT need to make is one of shame, disappointment, and disgust surrounding the toilet learning process. Keep your reactions neutral and matter of fact and they will adopt that same reaction.

In order to minimize your own stress and anxiety over accidents and the potential mess that can be made on furniture, some parents choose to either keep all activities for the day on the floor with a towel beneath the play space. Some parents even invest in some of the puppy pads that are available for dogs during crate training! These can even be put on furniture with regular bath towels over the top of them for both the added protection of your furniture against accidents and also for the extra comfort for your child! Be sure to do the same for the child's spot at the dining room table, as well. Mealtimes can sometimes be an extra tricky time for new potty learners to navigate paying attention to their bodily sensations and signals while enjoying their meals!

Day one will proceed with the fifteen-minute intervals to sit on the toilet, keeping it an experience that the child wants to have with reading, singing, or media watching every time they sit on the toilet. Many catchy little jingles have been created surrounding potty use and they are helpful because children love catchy, rhyming, sing-songs phrases to begin with, and delivering helpful potty information is a way of reinforcing the potty experience for them. If you don't want to use one that has already been made, make up one for your family that you know your child will enjoy!

During the course of this first day, any time your child does actually pee or poop in the toilet, be sure to make a giant fuss over this! You want your child to feel proud and accomplished and to always reinforce that experience of elimination on the toilet with celebration and acknowledgment.

Going to bed that evening, be sure to tell your little one how very proud of them that you are, even if they didn't pee or poop in the potty a single time. Explain to them that because they will be asleep and unable to tell when they need to go potty, you will be putting special training pants on them (NOT their regular diapers, but something absorbent like a pull up) but will begin their awesome work on the potty again in the morning. This training takes a lot out of children, so be prepared for your kid to sleep like a log!

A Quick Note About Nighttime Potty Training

After a long day of visiting the restroom every fifteen minutes, you and your child will be exhausted! It can be tempting to introduce nighttime training at the same time but do be aware that this is not really something that can be trained but rather just something that a child outgrows and develops into. If your child often wakes up from their naps and their nightly sleep stretches dry, then nighttime training and trials with underwear have a great shot at success! However, it is very rare for a child to be dry during naps and nighttime sleep stretches but unable to control their bladder during the day. Typically, bladder awareness and potty training come before nighttime dryness.

By the age of six, approximately 85% of children will be able to stay dry, but children can continue to have nighttime accidents on occasion up until the age of 12 without it being considered an area of concern. Parents and caregivers know their children best and will be able to determine if nighttime toilet training should begin at the same time.

If you do choose to go this route, you will essentially continue the interval training as you do during the day, only with longer lengths in between. Instead of every fifteen minutes, you will set your alarm for every three hours and will pick up your child (because they will be half-asleep!) and carry them in to sit on the toilet. Some parents use audio cues to help their children use the restroom in the middle of the night by turning on a nearby faucet. Once the child has gone to the potty, return them to their bed.

In order to decrease some of the time spent dealing with nighttime accidents, it will be important to use a waterproof mattress protector underneath the regular sheets. Some parents even choose to do additional layers of waterproof mattress protectors and sheets so that way when an accident occurs, the wet layers of sheets can be easily stripped away and there will be a dry layer already on the bed below. This can decrease nighttime sleep disruptions during the training process but do be aware that most nighttime potty training will be full of accidents if the child is not already mostly dry throughout the night. Again, this isn't really a training opportunity because nighttime bladder control has more to do with hormone production levels and those are produced on different timetables and have nothing to do with training.

Onward to Day Two!

Day two is much like day one, with one important difference. You will explain to your child that today, they will only be able to pick a treat out of the treasure box if they actually pee or poop in the potty. Do NOT mention accidents and be very careful about how you frame this information. You don't want your child to feel like they are being punished for having accidents, you want the emphasis to be on the reward for making it to the toilet!

Keep your spirits up and don't let up! This three-day potty training process is a *process,* not an event!

Day Three, Finally!

Day three is the day where big changes can often be seen. Explain to your child that today, you will be focusing on paying attention to your body and checking in. You will adjust your timer to half-hour increments, and rather than immediately traveling to the toilet to sit, you will instead encourage the "check-in."

"Let's stop and see if we need to go potty! <cue the gentle poking of the lower abdomen> Is there pee or poop in there that needs to come out? Should we go to try?" If it has been over an hour and your child still says they do not need the toilet and they have remained dry, encourage more drinking of fluids. Today is the day to really let your child figure out what these bodily sensations mean!

Chances are, your child is beginning to really connect the dots between what the feelings in their body mean and what they need to do about it. Day three is the day for them to really practice taking charge of this. You will still be checking in every half hour- and encouraging fluids- but you need to let them work out some of the cause and effect here, too.

Even if your child makes it to the toilet 100% on day 3, this does not mean that there will not be accidents moving forward! Small children are easily distracted and will still require some cueing and reminding the adults in their life. This is normal!

Read on for the next chapter if you find you have a Potty Training Outlier!

Chapter 3: Potty Training Outliers

Some children will potty train earlier than their peers and some will potty train later. This is just a normal part of this developmental process! If you have a child that has potty trained earlier than two, then you still may have some potty work coming in the future.

Potty training regression is when a child who was fully potty trained for a significant period of time begins having accidents consistently. If this is the case, you need to look at potential reasons why such as if there is an emotional or traumatic event occurring that needs addressed (toilet accidents are often present during times of abuse) or if extra support is needed day to day. Consult with your medical professional to rule out medical reasons such as a urinary tract infection or constipation.

For children who are beyond the age of four and still not interested in the potty or successful after an extended period of consistent potty training efforts, then this is also a scenario in which you might want to check in with a medical professional to see if there are any health issues at play that are causing the delay.

There are children who will potty train early and those that will potty train much later, but outliers exist on both ends and are typically not a cause for concern. Children who are not successful with potty training programs between the ages of two and four can spontaneously train themselves seemingly overnight when they decide that they are ready. Again, there is very little that children are able to have complete control over in their lives and the toileting process can be one of those things that children for reasons that adults may not understand. This does not mean your child is being manipulative or trying to be difficult; it means that they are trying to meet their own needs in the best way they know-how and support during this time means more emotional support than physical force.

Again, always speak to your child's doctor if you have any questions at all about health or well-being.

Bonus Chapter: Tips for Dads, From Dads

The relationship that a child has with their father is very unique and these are some tips and tricks that dads have shared with us:

"My little guy loves to do target practice in the toilet. I set him up with a few cheerios in the toilet and tell him to hit them as many times as he can and he is getting very good aim now!"

"My daughter loves to "show me how" so I like to pretend that I forgot how she uses the potty and she will walk me back to "show me how" and even sportscast the entire process!"

"I was worried about potty training and being away from home, but it's worked out really well so far. My son is really interested in all public restrooms, so anytime we end up at a store or restaurant, he immediately "has to go potty" which just means he wants to go see their restroom. It's working out though, not a single accident outside of the house!"

"Don't tell mom, but I still use Skittles. For pee on the potty, she gets two and for poop, she gets three. She never has an accident when I'm around."

"I let my daughter pick out a special foaming soap that she only gets to use after she's used the potty. It's sparkly blue and purple foam, so she makes sure that she makes it to the toilet so she can use some of her fancy "unicorn" soap!"

"I let my son pee in our backyard by our maple tree. We have a privacy fence so no one can see anything, and he LOVES it. I'm not sure what we will do in the winter, though..."

A lot of these dads have created playful ways to make the potty experience fun! Use your imagination to think of ways to do the same with your little one. Find ways to make this process tailored to you and your child and the this you like best.

Conclusion

Thank you for making it through to the end of **Potty Training in A Weekend:** *The Step-By-Step Guide to Potty Train Your Little Toddler in Less Than 3 Days. Perfect for Little Boys and Girls. Bonus Chapter with Tip for Careless Dads Included*, let's hope it was informative and able to provide you with all of the tools you need to achieve your goals in potty training your child.

Remember, potty training is a process and not an event. The three-day potty training method is intended to give your child a strong baseline knowledge of how to pay attention to and interpret the signals of their body and use the toilet properly. This doesn't mean that children will not have accidents as they go about their days, because children are easily distractible and after the fun of the three-day potty training method, going to sit on the potty won't seem quite as exciting as it did when they had a cheerleader on standby!

Continue to provide support for your child on their potty training journey and repeat the process as many times as you feel you need to. Remember that the potty training process requires a lot of your child: it is as much a cognitive process as it is a physical one. Be sure to tell your child each and every night that they are doing a great job in learning how to use the big kid potty and that you are proud of all their hard work. Children that feel supported for their efforts, even when their efforts don't yield perfect results, will be far more likely to persist with determination than a child that is given the signals that because they did not do something perfectly that they have failed.

If you have been consistently potty training for an extended period of time with no results, consult with your child's doctor to rule out any possible medical issues. If none are present, then consider pausing the potty training process and revisiting it later. Keep your child in the loop of what is happening with as neutral language as you can. A sample script might sound like, "It seems like maybe you aren't quite ready to begin the big kid potty yet. We will try again in one month, okay?" It isn't a failure, just a standard part of the process involved in this major developmental leap! Kids that seem resistant at first may just need a little while longer to fully understand and grow comfortable with the process.

Besides, you can always be rest assured that everyone learns how to use the potty eventually. You will not be sending your child off to college in diapers, guaranteed! Just as some kids walk later than others, some will potty train later, too. The day will come, believe it or not, you might even miss the days when your little one was in diapers.

Finally, if you found this book useful in any way, a review on Amazon is always appreciated!

CPSIA information can be obtained
at www.ICGtesting.com
Printed in the USA
BVHW040633100221
599639BV00031B/895